solidarity challenge

A 40-DAY JOURNEY

simple

CHARITY

To request permissions, contact the publisher at brian@simplecharity.org.

ISBN: 978-1-7359469-0-0

First paperback edition October 2020.

Edited by Angela Tawfik, Juliana Ryan, and Anna Faith Adair
Cover art by Angela Tawfik

Simple Charity
606 N Buchanan Blvd
Durham, NC 27701

Learn more at simplecharity.org

hi there

Dear friend,

It's an honor to introduce myself! My name is Brian, and I'm so glad that you are here.

I know that we just met, but I want to go out on a limb and ask an important question: How has your soul been lately? I ask because we at Simple Charity believe that followers of Jesus are called to walk in the way of Jesus, and that the way of Jesus leads to abundant life (John 10:10). And yet, how many of us experience that abundance day in and day out?

Human beings are wired to flourish when they connect with God. The practices articulated in this little book (gratitude, prayer, trust, giving and fasting) will help you connect with him. But only if you do them. This is not a normal book. The goal is not for you to read it and acquire new information. The goal is for you to practice new habits for 40 days and experience transformation.

The general structure of the Solidarity Challenge was mostly my design, but the daily devotionals were authored by my good friend Christopher Kuo, who also hosts Simple Charity's podcast, Two Coins, and is a sophomore at Duke University. We both received invaluable feedback from Angela Tawfik, Juliana Ryan and Anna Faith Adair.

This 40-day journey gets at the heart of why Simple Charity exists. If you would like to share your thoughts on the Solidarity Challenge, I would benefit greatly from your feedback. My email is brian@simplecharity.org. Feel free to drop me a note.

My prayer for you is that your intimacy with God grows over the next 40 days, that your love for the poor and the oppressed increases and that you experience the abundance of being hosted on this earth by the Giver of all gifts.

With gratitude,
Brian Grasso
Founder & CEO | Simple Charity

introduction

Read this introduction before beginning the *Solidarity Challenge* to learn about the virtue of solidarity.

Introduction

The moral tradition of virtue ethics was first articulated in its classic form by Aristotle in his famous work, *Nicomachean Ethics*. His argument basically went like this: Human beings have a unique purpose in the universe, or *telos*, which Aristotle believed was political in nature. Virtues are those qualities of a person, learned by habit and by heart, that orient a person towards the human *telos*.

Following the Aristotelian tradition, Alasdair MacIntyre in *After Virtue* focuses his definition of "virtue" on the goodness that is inherent in learning any kind of human excellence. For MacIntyre, a virtue is "an acquired human quality" that enables a person to learn a discipline such as philosophy, medicine, music or cricket (p. 191). He adds to this idea the importance of practicing virtues within a historical "tradition" (p. 223).

The Christian tradition gives us a much more refined understanding of our unique purpose in the world and therefore of the virtues. Christians believe that people were made to know, love and enjoy God. Not only that, Christians have a blueprint for the perfect human life in the person of Jesus, God's beloved Son.

After the New Testament was written, Christian thinkers throughout the ages like Augustine and Aquinas—and more recently, Tim Keller and Brian Fikkert—have reconciled aspects of Aristotle's thinking with the metaphysics of redemptive history. The two modern writers just named focus especially on the idea of *worship*. For Keller (in *Counterfeit Gods*) and Fikkert (in *Becoming Whole*), our habits show us what or whom we worship, and our worship shapes who we are.

This idea is spot on and should frame how Christians think about virtue. At the end of the day, the most important thing for us is to worship the one true God who has revealed himself through his written and incarnate Word. Virtues are those qualities that we work to develop in order to live lives that are pleasing to him. They are, simply put, character traits that honor God.

Solidarity Challenge

Virtues are always kinesthetic. By this, I mean that virtues always involve motion, adjustment and precision. Virtues are not sentiments. They are not feelings. They are habits learned by heart. Love looks very different in various circumstances, but a person who is *loving* knows the fine-tuned movements of love like a pianist knows the keys or a basketball player knows his free throw routine.

WHAT IS SOLIDARITY?

Solidarity is a biblical virtue. As with all Christian virtues, we see solidarity most clearly in the life of Jesus. One simple definition of solidarity is *unity regardless of proximity*. When Jesus was reigning on his throne in heaven, he expressed solidarity with humanity by becoming a human being like us. Jesus's moral life was not "proximate" to ours. He is perfect, and we are sinners. Nevertheless, Jesus embodied solidarity by unifying himself to his Church, paying our debt and sharing his riches.

The world is a shockingly unequal place. 40 million people woke up today entrapped in modern slavery. Hundreds of millions of people will not drink any safe, clean water today because they have no access to it. Tens of thousands of children under the age of five will die today from a preventable cause. Do these issues feel close or far?

For most of us living in America, these statistics on global human suffering feel distant from our day-to-day reality. That's where the virtue of solidarity comes in. God created *all* people in his image, and his love extends to *all* nations. Solidarity is a character trait that honors God because it acknowledges his heart. Psalm 34:18 teaches us that "The LORD is near to the brokenhearted."

The theological concept of the *imago Dei*—the image of God present in every human being, endowing each one of us with inestimable dignity and worth—is the basis for the Christian virtue of solidarity. As with all Christian virtues, solidarity is good and true and beautiful. It is a part of the abundant life. This book is designed to help you form habits to grow in this often forgotten yet wonderful virtue.

WHAT IS THE SOLIDARITY CHALLENGE?

Based on Simple Charity's *Profession of Practice* (see simplecharity.org/practice), the *Solidarity Challenge* is a 40-day journey to incorporate five new spiritual disciplines into your life. These five disciplines come from the Sermon on the Mount in Matthew 5-7. They are gratitude, prayer, trust, giving and fasting.

Throughout the next 35 days, you'll incorporate a new practice each week. During these weeks, focus on just one practice at a time. Don't get ahead of yourself. It's hard enough to form one new habit; it's too much to try to take on all five at once. That said, once a habit is there, keep it up even while adding the next. We'll spend the last five days of our journey together reflecting on how these habits produce abundance in our lives.

The *Solidarity Challenge* begins with the two daily practices: keeping a gratitude journal and praying the Lord's prayer. After that, we'll add a weekly liturgy of casting our burdens on the Lord. Then, we'll take on the life-giving practice of generosity. We'll end with a 24-hour fast. Don't worry: If you've never fasted before, we'll share some tips.

This journey is designed to make it as easy as possible to build new habits. Every day of your journey includes a Scripture passage, short devotional and prayer.

The purpose of the Solidarity Challenge is for you to "try on" these practices for a brief period, to prototype them in your life. If they fit, then keep them. If not, no worries. Along the way, if you mess up, have lots of grace for yourself. We have found that these are life-giving habits and believe that you will as well.

gratitude

This week, list three things that you are grateful for every day.

Read one daily devotional to reflect on the discipline of gratitude.

Gratitude in the Storm

*"And when he had said these things, he took bread, and giving
thanks to God in the presence of all he broke it and began to eat."*
(Acts 27:35)

It's easy to give thanks when the sun is shining, our grades
are top-notch or our salary is in the six figures. It's a lot harder
to be thankful when a family member gets sick or you lose your
job—or, in Paul's case, when your vessel has been caught in a
storm for two weeks and you're about to be shipwrecked.

In Acts 27, Paul is on a ship as a prisoner headed for Rome,
in chains for simply sharing the gospel. He'll be tried before the
Roman emperor, a man notorious for killing Christians. Then,
just when you're thinking that the situation couldn't get any
worse, the ship gets caught in a storm. The soldiers start tossing
the cargo; the sailors are so scared that they try to escape on one
of the lifeboats.

Caught in this catastrophic situation, Paul does something
both simple and astounding: he breaks bread and gives thanks.
"Rejoice always, pray without ceasing, give thanks *in all
circumstances*; for this is the will of God in Christ Jesus for you"
(1 Thess. 5:16-18; italics mine).

Gratitude is a discipline. We do disciplines (like exercise or
prayer) even when we don't feel like doing them—especially
when we don't feel like it—because we know that disciplines
form habits, and habits form our loves. Whatever our situation
today, God wills that we give thanks.

Even when all is stripped away, when the winds are raging
and the cargo is being tossed off the ship, we give thanks
because we know a God of unchanging goodness and grace. He
is faithful today, as he has been in the past. His mercies are new
every morning. "Give thanks to the Lord, for he is good, for his
steadfast love endures forever" (Ps. 136:1).

Solidarity Challenge

Unchanging God, thank you for your goodness. Thank you for your steadfast love. Teach me to rejoice in all circumstances and to give thanks in the storm. Amen.

Further reading: Psalm 34:17-18; Psalm 119:50, 52; Isaiah 4:6.

Today I am grateful for:

1.

2.

3.

Gratitude

The Father of Lights

"He himself gives to all mankind life and breath and everything."
(Acts 17:25b)

Independence kills gratitude. When we think that the good things in our lives are earned by our own effort, we'll have a hard time honestly saying "thank you" to the Lord. If we don't see life as a gift, we'll never thank God for it.

According to Scripture, our very breath is a gift from the Lord. We are alive this particular day because the Lord sustains every cell in our bodies: "In him all things hold together" (Col. 1:17). Just as life is a gift, so are our talents, network and financial resources. "You shall remember the Lord your God, for it is he who gives you power to get wealth" (Deut. 8:18). Even our salvation is an undeserved gift: "For by grace you have been saved through faith. And this is not your own doing; it is the gift of God" (Eph. 2:8). Scripture is clear: we receive all good things from the hand of God. "Every good gift and every perfect gift is from above, coming down from the Father of lights, with whom there is no variation or shadow due to change" (James 1:17).

Thankfulness flows from a prayer of dependence: "Give us this day our daily bread." Our gratitude takes on new meaning when we recognize that all we are and all we have is from the Lord. For many of us, that's a foreign concept. But for our brothers and sisters in Christ who live in material poverty around the world, this truth is a lived reality. They take each mouthful of food as a gift.

Dependence fosters gratitude, but gratitude also gives rise to dependence. That may be why God commands us again and again to give thanks. When we express our thankfulness, we enter into a deeper reliance on the Lord, our Savior and Sustainer. "In him we live and move and have our being" (Acts 17:28).

Solidarity Challenge

Holy Father, I praise you for you are the Sustainer of all things, including myself. Thank you for your work in my life, your blessings and gifts. All that I have is from you. Nurture in me a spirit of childlike dependence on you. Amen.

Further reading: Acts 17:22-34; John 15:1-8.

Today I am grateful for:

1.

2.

3.

DAY THREE

Fighting for Joy

"Out of them shall come songs of thanksgiving, and the voices of those who celebrate." (Jer. 30:19)

All of us want more joy in our lives. We start our mornings hoping that we'll be happier than before. But we soon get steamrolled by the reality of life: the struggles, disappointments and regrets endemic to our daily lives. Joy feels just out of reach.

In biblical terms, cultivating joy takes discipline: intentional practice and dedicated rhythms of life. We must fight for joy, as John Piper puts it. And one way we fight for joy is through the discipline of gratitude.

Thinking of gratitude as a discipline both frees and convicts us. On the one hand, if gratitude is a discipline, then we know gratitude isn't about simply having feelings of positivity. Some of us are naturally less positive and sunny than others, and God doesn't ask us to manufacture feelings. At the same time, seeing gratitude as a discipline should challenge us. We can and should develop gratitude through intentional effort and practices. As disciples of Jesus, we have no excuse for thanklessness. Through intentional habits—like writing down or verbalizing what we're thankful for every day—and by the Spirit's power, we cultivate hearts of gratitude.

As we grow in gratitude, we also grow in joy. As pastor Steve Fuller points out, throughout Scripture, joy and gratitude are inextricably linked. Psalm 95:2 declares, "Let us come into his presence with thanksgiving; let us make a joyful noise to him with songs of praise." Thankfulness leads to deeper joy in God and in his gifts.

Do you want to experience joy today? Take time to give thanks.

Joyous God, you alone bring true joy. I thank you for the gift of gratitude. Please help me to rejoice always and to give thanks in all circumstances. Amen.

Solidarity Challenge

Further reading: Psalm 95; Psalm 97.

Today I am grateful for:

1.

2.

3.

The Doldrums

"I know how to be brought low, and I know how to abound. In any and every circumstance, I have learned the secret of facing plenty and hunger, abundance and need." (Phil. 4:12)

There's a narrow belt of water around the Equator dreaded by sailors. Officially, it's known as the Inter-Tropical Convergence Zone. Unofficially, it's known to sailors as the "doldrums." Because of the convergence of various wind patterns, the "doldrums" have very little surface wind, and sailing ships can get stranded in the stretch of water for weeks. Calm waters can be as perilous as stormy ones.

For Christians, the doldrums of life are a dangerous place. Often, the greatest trial comes in a form we least expect: abundant wealth, a healthy marriage and a successful career. When we reach the pinnacle of worldly success, we're in grave danger of worshipping the things of the world instead of God, of making our home here instead of looking to our future city. Peace and prosperity can undo us.

Moses warned the Israelites of this temptation as they stood on the brink of the Promised Land. "When the LORD your God brings you into the land that he swore to your fathers ... with great and good cities that you did not build, and houses full of all good things that you did not fill ... and when you eat and are full, then take care lest you forget the LORD" (Deut. 6:10-12). Moses knew that calm waters are conducive to spiritual apathy.

Thankfulness reminds us that all we are and all we have comes from above. The key to maintaining spiritual vitality during times of abundance is to orient our hearts toward the Lord through the discipline of gratitude.

By giving thanks, we fight pride and embrace dependence. We keep our attention fixed on Jesus; we practice contentment. Gratitude puts the wind back in our sails.

Solidarity Challenge

Steadfast Father, you are good in the tough times and in the easy times. I confess that my heart is so prone to wander. I so easily forget you amid all of your blessings. Please keep my heart fixed on you both when I am brought low and when I abound. Amen.

Further reading: Philippians 4:16-20; Deuteronomy 6.

Today I am grateful for:

1.

2.

3.

Gratitude Glasses

"Enter his gates with thanksgiving and his courts with praise!"
(Psalm 100:4)

"Gratitude is like glasses," according to pastor Steve Fuller. Gratitude helps us see God more clearly. When we give thanks, we remember our position as creatures—fearfully and wonderfully made, but creatures nonetheless. We refocus on the Creator who is holy and all-powerful, the Father of lights who is the source of every good and perfect gift. We thank God for his earthly gifts, but we also thank God for the greatest gift of all—himself.

That's why gratitude ultimately flows into praise. Thanksgiving leads us from the gift to the Giver, overflowing in adoration. C. S. Lewis makes this point in *Letters to Malcolm*: "Gratitude exclaims ... 'How good of God to give me this.' Adoration says, 'What must be the quality of that Being whose far-off and momentary coruscations are like this!' One's mind runs back up the sunbeam to the sun."

Praise and thanksgiving are repeatedly linked in the Psalms. Psalm 95:1-2 says, "Oh come, let us sing to the LORD; let us make a joyful noise to the rock of our salvation! Let us come into his presence with thanksgiving; let us make a joyful noise to him with songs of praise!" "I give you thanks, O LORD, with my whole heart; before the gods I sing your praise" (Ps. 138:1-2). "I will give to the LORD the thanks due to his righteousness, and I will sing praise to the name of the LORD, the Most High" (Ps. 7:17).

It would be a grave mistake for us to stop at the gift without praising the Giver. The sunbeam is a sore replacement for the sun. Today, let us enter his gates with thanksgiving and his courts with praise.

Father God, I praise you for you are the Giver of life, my Sustainer and Savior. Thank you for your care for every detail of my life.

17

Solidarity Challenge

Thank you for your gifts. But, more than anything you give, I take joy in you. Amen.

Further reading: Psalm 100.

Today I am grateful for:

1.

2.

3.

Every Now is an Eternity

"Be still, and know that I am God." (Ps. 46:10)

We are a hurried people. We dash from meeting to meeting, from notification to notification. We are constantly checking and endlessly diverted. In his book *The Ruthless Elimination of Hurry*, John Mark Comer, following Dallas Willard, describes hurry as *the* great enemy of spiritual life. In this technology-infused world, our efficiency and connectivity have increased, but at what cost to our souls?

Hurry has robbed us of intimacy with the present. But the present is where God intends for us to dwell. Comer says this: "Life isn't 'out there' in the next dopamine hit, the next task, the next experience; it's right here, now. As Frank Laubach...so beautifully said, 'Every now is an eternity if it is full of God.'"

Gratitude draws us back to the present. Gratitude forces us to slow down, to pause, to carve out time in the day to breathe and to give thanks. As we grow in thanksgiving, we practice new, slower rhythms of life. It's hard to notice God's gifts when we are perpetually in a hurry.

C. S. Lewis drew the connection between gratitude and being present in *The Screwtape Letters*, his fictional depiction of a demon instructing his apprentice:

> "The humans live in time but our Enemy [Jesus] destines them to eternity. He therefore, I believe, wants them to attend chiefly to two things, to eternity itself, and to that point of time which they call the Present. For the Present is the point at which time touches eternity. ... He would therefore have them continually concerned with eternity (which means being concerned with Him) or with the Present ... obeying the present voice of conscience, bearing the present cross, receiving the present grace, *giving thanks* for the present pleasure" (italics mine).

Solidarity Challenge

Father, you have destined me for eternity and have given me the gift of the present. I'm so prone to worry about the future and miss your present gifts. I choose today to slow down, to wait, to rest, to give thanks. Amen.

Further reading: Psalm 46.

Today I am grateful for:

1.

2.

3.

Eucharisteo

"He fell on his face at Jesus's feet, giving him thanks. Now he was a Samaritan." (Luke 17:16)

Jesus was on his way to Jerusalem when he passed by ten lepers, who cried out to him for healing. Jesus showed mercy and healed them, but only one of the ten returned to thank him: "Were not ten cleansed? Where are the nine? Was no one found to return and give praise to God except this foreigner?"

Each of us was once a leper, our hearts marred by the disease of sin. In Jesus, we found healing. He replaced our hearts of stone with hearts of flesh. He made us new creations. This is the miracle of salvation: the old has gone, the new has come.

And yet, we are so prone to forget. Like the nine lepers, we so often continue our lives without thanking God for his "inexpressible gift." We grumble and complain when we could be leaping for joy over God's salvation.

That is why spiritual practices like communion are so vital—they break through our spiritual amnesia. When we break the bread and drink the wine, we receive again the sacrifice of Jesus Christ. We remember the One who gave thanks before bleeding on a Roman cross: "And he took a cup, and when he had given thanks he gave it to them, saying, 'Drink of it, all of you'" (Matt. 26:27). The Greek word used here for "given thanks" is *eucharisteo*. To practice the Eucharist is to give thanks for the ultimate sacrifice.

But thanksgiving doesn't end with the Sunday benediction. We must be *eucharisteo* people, disciples defined by thanksgiving. Each new morning, we wake forgiven and set free—healed of our leprosy—because of the body and blood of Jesus Christ. He gave thanks on the night of his crucifixion, and so we too give thanks as we take up our own crosses and die to ourselves. We give thanks because he gave us himself.

Solidarity Challenge

Crucified Savior, thank you for your sacrifice on my behalf, your life-giving body broken and your precious blood shed for me. Thank you that I can now come before the Father with peace and boldness because of your death and resurrection. Today, Jesus, I dedicate my life as an offering of gratitude to you. Amen.

Further reading: Matthew 26:26-29.

Today I am grateful for:

1.

2.

3.

prayer

This week, pray the Lord's prayer daily. You can find the Lord's prayer in Matthew 6:9-13.

Add this new practice while maintaining your daily discipline of gratitude.

Read one daily devotional to go deeper in your understanding of the Lord's prayer.

Solidarity Challenge

The Father's Lap

"Our Father in heaven" (Matt. 6:9b)

Here we find an answer to the question lurking behind every prayer: who are we really praying to?

God our Father—that's the answer. The God who spun the galaxies into existence and calls each star by name, who crafts the snowflakes and calms the winds with a word.

Our Father. It's easy to miss the revolutionary nature of this phrase. None of the great prophets and kings of the Old Testament—not even David, arguably the most prolific "prayer" of the Bible—called God "Father." But then comes a wandering Rabbi named Jesus: "Pray then like this," he tells us. "Father" was Jesus's favorite word for God. And through faith in this Jesus, we become the Father's children, "born, not of blood nor of the will of the flesh nor of the will of man, but of God" (John 1:13).

A good father delights to hear his child's prattling, laughter, fears and desires; he rejoices in being able to give good gifts to his children. Jesus says as much in the Sermon on the Mount: "Which one of you, if his son asks him for bread, will give him a stone?" (Matt. 7:9). If human fathers listen to and care for their children, then how much more will the heavenly Father hear us when we pray? All human fathers have flaws in one form or another, but this Father is good to the very core of his being. And he waits eagerly for his children to pray.

Father in heaven, I rejoice that you are my Father and I am your child. I don't deserve your love, and yet you shower me with your attention. You are so, so good. Amen.

Further reading: Luke 11:1-13; 1 John 3:1-3.

Prayer

Today I am grateful for:

1.

2.

3.

Our Father in heaven, hallowed be your name. Your kingdom come, your will be done, on earth as it is in heaven. Give us this day our daily bread, and forgive us our debts, as we also have forgiven our debtors. And lead us not into temptation, but deliver us from evil.

Solidarity Challenge

The Invasion

"Hallowed be your name" (Matt. 6:9)

Most of us have to reach for Merriam-Webster when we come across this line. What does it mean for God's name to be *hallowed*? And why his *name*?

To hallow God's name is to sanctify it, to treat it as holy, to show reverence. A name, in the full Jewish sense, encompasses a person's character and attributes—their entire being. We are really praying then for God to be glorified, for his Name to be exalted in our lives, in our country, in our world.

It's no coincidence that this is the first request of the Lord's prayer. When we pray these words, we acknowledge that God is the greatest Treasure of our lives and that every other prayer—for the kingdom, for bread or for forgiveness—flows from this one. We are asking God to orient ourselves towards him. To carve out a space at the very core of our beings and to flood it with his holy presence. To make our souls cry out: "Your name and remembrance are the desire of our soul" (Isa. 26:8).

But this prayer is as wide and all-encompassing as it is deep. The Apostle Paul tells us: "Whether you eat or drink, or whatever you do, do all to the glory of God" (1 Cor. 10:31). Our entire purpose, according to the Westminster Catechism, is to "glorify God and enjoy him forever." This prayer should permeate our everyday lives. In our groggy mornings, *hallowed be your name*. In our nine to five, *hallowed be your name*. In our cooking and walking and eating and sleeping, *hallowed be your name*. This prayer is a daily incarnation, the invasion of the magnificent into the mundane.

Reflecting on these words, John Piper once wrote this in his journal:

Lord, grant that I would, in all my weaknesses and limitations, remain close to the one clear, grand theme of my life: Your magnificence. Amen.

Prayer

Further reading: 1 Corinthians 10:23-32; Isaiah 26:1-21.

Today I am grateful for:

1.

2.

3.

Our Father in heaven, hallowed be your name. Your kingdom come, your will be done, on earth as it is in heaven. Give us this day our daily bread, and forgive us our debts, as we also have forgiven our debtors. And lead us not into temptation, but deliver us from evil.

Solidarity Challenge

The Mustard Seed

"Your kingdom come" (Matt. 6:10)

The entire biblical saga is the story of a King inaugurating his kingdom. This story begins in Genesis 3, where Adam and Eve—the King's first subjects—rebel by eating the forbidden fruit. Cast out of the garden, Adam and Eve are the first in a long line of people, from Babel to Babylon, who attempt to build their own kingdoms apart from God.

But the King doesn't give up on his people or his kingdom. The rest of the Bible tells the story of God establishing the kingdom of heaven on earth, beginning with his chosen people of Israel, a "kingdom of priests and a holy nation" (Ex. 19:6). Eventually, the King himself comes to earth—born not in a Roman palace but in the humble town of Bethlehem. Jesus's first words recorded in the gospel of Mark were these: "The time is fulfilled, and the kingdom of God is at hand; repent and believe in the gospel" (Mark 1:15).

Jesus's inauguration of the kingdom of heaven means several things. It means the fulfillment of God's Old Testament promises to save his people. It means tangible things as well: the healing of the sick, care for the poor, justice for the oppressed. And it means the arrival of Jesus's rule and reign over our hearts, established decisively by his death and resurrection and the outpouring of his Spirit.

At the same time, we live in a world that remains broken and bleeding, a world plagued by war, rape, disease and poverty. Though the kingdom has been inaugurated, it won't be consummated until Jesus returns in all of his glory. And so, when we pray "Your kingdom come," we are making a truly audacious request. We're praying for God to heal the diseased, bind up the brokenhearted and enact justice for the oppressed. We're praying that he would set hearts on fire for himself. We're praying that God would turn a mustard seed into a massive tree. And, because we are his "kingdom of priests," we're asking that God would do those things through us.

Father, thank you for choosing me, a broken vessel, to be your instrument in advancing your kingdom. Lord, let your kingdom come, in my heart, in this country, in this world. Come soon, Lord Jesus. Amen.

Further reading: Matthew 4:12-17; Matthew 13:31-33.

Today I am grateful for:

1.

2.

3.

Our Father in heaven, hallowed be your name. Your kingdom come, your will be done, on earth as it is in heaven. Give us this day our daily bread, and forgive us our debts, as we also have forgiven our debtors. And lead us not into temptation, but deliver us from evil.

Solidarity Challenge

The Throne

"Your will be done" (Matt. 6:10)

Every sin makes a statement: "My will be done." When we sin, we're saying that self, not God, is on the throne of our lives, dictating our actions and passions. In a world that idolizes self-promotion, it's far too easy for us to try to chart our own destiny. This kind of self-exaltation doesn't require a radical declaration of commitment. All it takes is an accumulation of thousands of moments—moments that translate into days, and days that translate into a life—where we choose our will instead of God's.

Jesus knows this about us. That's why he gives us this prayer. He invites us into a posture of daily surrender, where, relinquishing our illusion of control, we allow God to mold our hearts and lives according to his design.

Jesus prayed this prayer at the most agonizing moment of his life. Kneeling in the Garden of Gethsemane, knowing the brutal baptism he would soon undergo, he cried these words: "Abba, Father, all things are possible for you. Remove this cup from me. Yet not what I will, but what you will" (Mark 14:36).

Like all prayer, this request molds our hearts and leads to action. To pray, "Your will be done" while still living out our own wills is a dangerous game to play with the God of the universe. After praying, Jesus carried out the Father's will by submitting to the crown of thorns. In doing so, he took the punishment we deserved for all the countless times we've crowned self instead of God. Following his example, we take up our own crosses, dying daily to self and living more fully for God.

Father, your will be done in my life. Take me as I am, with my wayward heart, my rebellious will. Shape me, refine me, transform me into your Son's likeness. Amen.

Further reading: Mark 14:32-42; Romans 12:1-2.

Prayer

Today I am grateful for:

1.

2.

3.

Our Father in heaven, hallowed be your name. Your kingdom come, your will be done, on earth as it is in heaven. Give us this day our daily bread, and forgive us our debts, as we also have forgiven our debtors. And lead us not into temptation, but deliver us from evil.

Solidarity Challenge

A Prayer of Solidarity

"Give us this day our daily bread" (Matt. 6:11)

This can feel like a strange prayer to make when we have packed coolers and full fridges. What does it mean to ask for our "daily bread" when we're already planning for a comfortable retirement?

On one level, this prayer reminds us that all we have, including the food in our refrigerators, is part of God's provision for us. Even those things we take for granted—clean water, comfortable housing, three meals a day—are given to us from the hand of God. "Every good and perfect gift is from above, coming down from the Father of lights" (James 1:17). Paul puts it more bluntly: "What do you have that you did not receive?" (1 Cor. 4:7). This prayer helps us celebrate the simple, oft-overlooked things.

On another level, this prayer is also an expression of solidarity. Around the world, millions are mired in hunger and economic poverty, including many of our brothers and sisters in Christ. For these people, the prayer for daily bread is a cry for survival. And so, when we pray these words, we remember such people and ask God to provide for their needs just as he's provided for ours.

The more we grow in thankfulness for God's daily gifts, the more we are able to give freely and joyfully to others. We channel our resources to help provide for those without bread or water or money. As we do so, we discover a wonderful mystery of the kingdom: God uses us to be his answers to prayer.

Father of lights, I thank you for the many gifts you have given. I confess how often I take them for granted. Lord, give us this day our daily bread. And thank you for Jesus, the living bread who nourishes us. Help us to leverage our time and talents to provide for those without bread today. Amen.

Prayer

Further reading: James 1:16-18.

Today I am grateful for:

1.

2.

3.

Our Father in heaven, hallowed be your name. Your kingdom come, your will be done, on earth as it is in heaven. Give us this day our daily bread, and forgive us our debts, as we also have forgiven our debtors. And lead us not into temptation, but deliver us from evil.

Solidarity Challenge

Compelled by the Cross

"And forgive us our debts, as we also have forgiven our debtors"
(Matt. 6:12)

Most of us readily admit that we sin every day and need God's forgiveness. But the real shocking part of this prayer is the second clause: "As we also have forgiven our debtors." At the end of the Lord's Prayer, Jesus says, "For if you forgive others their trespasses, your heavenly Father will also forgive you, but if you do not forgive others their trespasses, neither will your Father forgive your trespasses" (Matt. 6:14-15).

We know that God's forgiveness is an undeserved gift, not a result of works (Eph. 2:8-9). But the way in which we treat people who have wronged us is evidence of God's transforming presence in our hearts. Forgiven people forgive others.

This echoes a parable Jesus once told his disciples. A servant owes a king ten thousand talents (one talent was equivalent to 20 years' worth of wages). When the servant can't pay the debt, the king waives the entire sum. But then the servant goes to one of his own debtors, a man who owes him a hundred denarii (a denarii was one day's wage). Seizing the man, he imprisons him until he can repay the money. When the king hears about this, he's furious with the servant: "Should not you have had mercy on your fellow servant, as I had mercy on you?" (Matt. 18:33).

We owe a debt to God that's far greater than any debt owed by others to us. And yet God doesn't treat us as our sins deserve, for, while we were his enemies, Christ died for us. The cross enables us to boldly approach a holy God and to pray "forgive us our debts." And it's the cross that compels us to offer that same forgiveness to others.

Father of mercies, thank you for your forgiveness, bought with the precious blood of your Son Jesus. I confess to you all the times where I've harbored a grudge in my heart. Teach me to forgive as you have daily forgiven me. Amen.

Prayer

Further reading: Matthew 18:21-35; Romans 5:1-11.

Today I am grateful for:

1.

2.

3.

Our Father in heaven, hallowed be your name. Your kingdom come, your will be done, on earth as it is in heaven. Give us this day our daily bread, and forgive us our debts, as we also have forgiven our debtors. And lead us not into temptation, but deliver us from evil.

The Battle

"And lead us not into temptation, but deliver us from evil" (Matt. 6:13)

We're soldiers. We battle against "spiritual forces of evil in the heavenly places" (Eph. 6:12). But we also battle the mundane temptations in the everyday, earthly places—in our workplaces, in our schools, in our bedrooms when no one is watching.

This final petition of the Lord's Prayer reminds us of this battle. As we make this prayer, we cultivate a spirit of vigilance. How easy it is to go about our days with a spirit of apathy, forgetting that the cosmic clash between good and evil is playing out today, in this ordinary moment. There are no ordinary days. "Stay awake," Jesus said, time after time, and this prayer prods us from our slumber. We are to be "sober-minded" and "watchful," for our "adversary the devil prowls around like a roaring lion, seeking someone to devour" (1 Pet. 5:8).

And yet, we have nothing to fear, for we worship a God of unfathomable power and unchanging goodness—a God who goes out to battle with us. "The Lord will fight for you" (Exod. 14:14). "'Not by might, nor by power, but by my Spirit,' says the LORD of hosts" (Zech. 4:6). "If God is for us, who can be against us?" (Rom. 8:31). And so, this prayer, like all prayer, is an expression of dependence. We cannot wage this war on our own strength, and we don't have to. We are indwelt with the Spirit of Jesus Christ, our great Captain who sustains us, strengthens us and protects us from evil. We fight this battle from our knees.

As we do so we rest assured knowing that Christ has already claimed the ultimate triumph on the Cross. We are his, and no one can snatch us from his hand. "In all these things, we are more than conquerors through him who loved us" (Rom. 8:37).

Prayer

Mighty God, thank you that you go out to battle on my behalf. Lord, outfit me with all your spiritual armor and deliver me from evil and temptation today. Let me sing over my enemies. Amen.

Further reading: Ephesians 6:10-20; 2 Chronicles 20:1-30.

Today I am grateful for:

1.

2.

3.

Our Father in heaven, hallowed be your name. Your kingdom come, your will be done, on earth as it is in heaven. Give us this day our daily bread, and forgive us our debts, as we also have forgiven our debtors. And lead us not into temptation, but deliver us from evil.

trust

Right now, list three things that you are anxious about and pray to God about them, out loud if you are able. Then, read Philippians 4:6–7:

Do not be anxious about anything, but in everything by prayer and supplication with thanksgiving let your requests be made known to God. And the peace of God, which surpasses all understanding, will guard your hearts and your minds in Christ Jesus.

Continue to maintain your daily practices of gratitude and prayer.

Read one daily devotional to reflect on the faithfulness of God and grow in trust.

Trust

The Promises

"But if God so clothes the grass of the field, which today is alive and tomorrow is thrown into the oven, will he not much more clothe you, O you of little faith?" (Matt. 6:30)

Jesus's command that we "do not worry" may be both his simplest and his hardest. Worry is our default. We worry about everything from bothersome details to global catastrophes: lost keys, warming seas and proliferating viruses. We worry because we want to maintain a mirage of control over our lives. And even though worrying accomplishes nothing—"Can any one of you by worrying add a single hour to your life?"—we do it anyway.

Worry, according to Jesus, is rooted in faithlessness ("you of little faith"). In this passage, Jesus assures us that God is a good Father who cares about our every need and promises to provide. The greatest weapon against worry is trust in the promises of God. And what are those promises?

He knows our needs (Matt. 6:32). He knows every hair on our heads (Luke 12:7). He will never leave us nor forsake us (Heb. 13:5). He invites us to cast all our anxieties upon him, because he cares for us (1 Pet. 5:7). He is all-powerful, and no purpose of his can be thwarted (Job 42:2). He will meet all our needs according to the riches of his glory in Christ Jesus (Phil. 4:19). He works all things together for good in the lives of those who love him (Rom. 8:28). He chose us in his love and mercy before the foundation of the world (Eph. 1:4).

We fight worry with faith—faith in God and in his truth. To the degree we believe and internalize his promises, our worry recedes. God calls us to live radically and faithfully in the present, surrendering our worries and seeking first his kingdom. His abundant life awaits.

Prince of Peace, thank you for your promises to provide. I confess how often I give in to worry, how often I doubt you and your word. I surrender all of my worries to you today. Please guard my heart and mind with your peace. Amen.

Further reading: Luke 12:4-7; Matthew 6:25-34.

Today I am grateful for:

1.

2.

3.

Our Father in heaven, hallowed be your name. Your kingdom come, your will be done, on earth as it is in heaven. Give us this day our daily bread, and forgive us our debts, as we also have forgiven our debtors. And lead us not into temptation, but deliver us from evil.

Trust

In Everything

"Do not be anxious about anything, but in everything by prayer and supplication with thanksgiving let your requests be made known to God." (Phil. 4:6-7)

No worry of ours is too small or too large for God. This verse banishes any self-justification we give for our anxieties. "Do not be anxious about anything," Paul says, and that includes our college tuition and our final papers, the health of our marriage and the number of followers we've accumulated on Instagram. God intends his peace to permeate every nook and cranny of our lives.

Instead of stewing in our anxiety, we're called to lay our worries before the Lord and to invite him to act on our behalf. To ask God to intervene in our everyday lives is to acknowledge our own inadequacy apart from him. As Jesus makes clear in John 15, we are the branches; he is the vine. We can do nothing apart from him. But presenting our requests to God also flows from trust in his character. We surrender our worries with confidence in God's power and goodness. He can do abundantly more than we can ever ask or imagine, according to his power at work within us (Eph. 3:20). He is a good Father who delights to give good gifts to his children (Luke 11:13).

But we go beyond merely presenting our requests to God. We also give thanks. Like Samuel of the Old Testament, we raise an Ebenezer stone, declaring, "Till now the Lord has helped us" (1 Sam. 7:12). We remember all the ways God has faithfully dealt with our past worries and anxieties. And we thank him for his present gifts: a full stomach, family and friends, a night of rest. (One of the chief problems with worrying is that it distracts us from being faithful in the present and taking joy in the immediate.) We also thank the Lord for the future, trusting that he will work all things together for our good and for his glory.

Solidarity Challenge

When we accept God's invitation to surrender our every worry, he promises that his peace will guard our hearts and our minds. God's peace is a fortress that protects our hearts and our minds—the core of our being—from the marauding armies of worry. God is our refuge and our strength. All he asks of us is that we be still (Ps. 46:10).

Father in heaven, I want to know your peace in my life. I confess that I am so often caught up in my anxieties and worries. I surrender all of them to you today. Take me as I am and fill me with your presence and peace. Amen.

Further reading: 1 Samuel 7; Philippians 4.

Today I am grateful for:

1.

2.

3.

Our Father in heaven, hallowed be your name. Your kingdom come, your will be done, on earth as it is in heaven. Give us this day our daily bread, and forgive us our debts, as we also have forgiven our debtors. And lead us not into temptation, but deliver us from evil.

Mist

"What is your life? For you are a mist that appears for a little time and then vanishes." (James 4:14)

At the root of our worry is our infatuation with control. Our culture has led us to believe that we are the captains of our own vessels, sovereigns over our own kingdoms. Everywhere we turn, from advertisements to university orientation sessions, we encounter the same message—the same deception—that we can decide our own fates and be whoever we want to be.

God paints a different picture in Scripture. Now, of course, we do have agency in our lives; our choices are real and meaningful. And yet, too often we ignore the many ways in which we lack control. We didn't determine our family or our genetic makeup. We can't control the political trajectory of our country, the state of the stock market, or the safety and health of our loved ones. We can't prevent a new virus from mutating and proliferating across the globe. Ultimately, we can't control the length of our days. We are frail creatures. To be human is to embrace our limitations and lack of control.

Coming to terms with this illusion of control can be scary. One response is to descend more deeply into worry. A better response is to take refuge in the One who is in complete control.

God controls the events of history. He makes kingdoms rise and fall. He has power over life and death. And God is also sovereign over the intimate details of our lives. We trust that his almighty power is working in our lives, orchestrating every detail according to his good purposes.

We can take comfort in these truths. If I'm the decider of my own destiny, then everything depends on my actions. There is no room for failure. But God weaves even our mistakes into the beautiful tapestry of our lives.

Solidarity Challenge

Almighty God, I praise you for you are always in control. You are sovereign and good. Help me to surrender my life to you, to stop believing the lie that I'm sovereign. You are my King. Amen.

Further reading: James 4:13-17.

Today I am grateful for:

1.

2.

3.

Our Father in heaven, hallowed be your name. Your kingdom come, your will be done, on earth as it is in heaven. Give us this day our daily bread, and forgive us our debts, as we also have forgiven our debtors. And lead us not into temptation, but deliver us from evil.

Trust

Heart Check

"Those who make them become like them; so do all who trust in them." (Ps. 115:8)

Worry is a barometer for our hearts. What we worry about reveals what we trust—what we depend on for our security, joy and peace. We worry about how we appear to others because we depend on people's approval for our self-worth. We worry over our money because we trust in finances for our security. We worry about our relationships because we depend on loved ones for happiness. Worry shows us where our ultimate trust resides.

Trust is intimately wrapped up in worship. As Tim Keller explains in *Counterfeit Gods*, the Bible uses three words to portray worship: love, trust and obey. Whatever we look to for our ultimate security—whatever we trust—becomes our god, and we are shaped into its likeness. Anything can become an idol, a counterfeit god. In Psalm 115, Scripture exposes the futility of trusting in idols. Idols are the work of human hands. They have no power to save or protect us. In contrast, God is our "help" and our "shield."

God alone deserves our trust. All other things are temporary or changing. Money doesn't last beyond the grave, and a life's savings can be wiped out by a financial crisis. People's approval is fickle. Our physical beauty and strength will inevitably fade with time. In contrast, "Jesus Christ is the same yesterday and today and forever" (Heb. 13:8). Only this unchanging, all-satisfying God can sustain the weight of our hearts.

Trusting in idols always breeds worry. Trusting and delighting in God produces peace. Where are you placing your trust today?

Holy and Immortal God, you alone deserve worship. Not to us but to your name be the glory. Lead me into deeper worship of yourself. Help me to trust in you alone. Amen.

Solidarity Challenge

Further reading: Psalm 115.

Today I am grateful for:

1.

2.

3.

Our Father in heaven, hallowed be your name. Your kingdom come, your will be done, on earth as it is in heaven. Give us this day our daily bread, and forgive us our debts, as we also have forgiven our debtors. And lead us not into temptation, but deliver us from evil.

Weighed Down

"Cast your burden on the LORD, and he will sustain you" (Ps. 55:22)

New Testament writers often use the analogy of a race to portray the Christian life. In 1 Corinthians 9:24, Paul says, "Do you not know that in a race all the runners run, but only one receives the prize? So run that you may obtain it." The writer of Hebrews tells us to "run with endurance the race that is set before us." When you run a race, you want to be as lightweight as possible. The Christian life is a marathon, not a sprint. Imagine trying to run a marathon while carrying a 30-pound dumbbell.

Worry weighs us down. We've all experienced the heaviness of heart that comes from anxiety. When we worry, we're less present to our family and friends, less joyful and kind, less free. Worry keeps us from running the race God has set before us. Worry robs us of abundance.

But we were never meant to bear this burden. Scripture uses the image of physically throwing off our burdens to demonstrate what it means to surrender our worries to God. "Cast your burden on the LORD" (Ps. 55:22). "Casting all your anxieties on him, because he cares for you" (1 Pet. 5:7). In Hebrews, we are called to "lay aside every weight, and sin which clings so closely" (12:1). Instead of worrying, we fix our eyes on Jesus, the One who lived and died on our behalf.

In *The Pilgrim's Progress* by John Bunyan, Christian starts his journey with a massive burden on his back. Then, when he sees the cross, the burden falls from his back and rolls into an empty tomb. This allegory illustrates how we lose the burden of guilt and condemnation when we put our trust in Christ, but it also provides an image for our everyday Christian lives. Daily we return to Christ and lay our burdens—our worries, frailties and anxieties—at the foot of the cross. Christ's yoke is easy, and his burden is light.

Solidarity Challenge

Liberating God, thank you that you invite me to cast my burdens on you. I surrender all of my worries now, both great and small, into your loving hands. Thank you for caring for me. Amen.

Further reading: Hebrews 12:1-2; 1 Corinthians 9:24-27.

Today I am grateful for:

1.

2.

3.

Our Father in heaven, hallowed be your name. Your kingdom come, your will be done, on earth as it is in heaven. Give us this day our daily bread, and forgive us our debts, as we also have forgiven our debtors. And lead us not into temptation, but deliver us from evil.

Trust

The Lord is my Helper

"He will not leave you or forsake you" (Deut. 31:6)

Worry spells the death of generosity. When we worry about our future and our finances, we cling to our money, refusing to give or surrender to God. Money becomes our source of security, our downpayment against the unpredictability of life. Worry leaves us with closed hearts and clenched fists.

In contrast, deep trust in the Lord leads to generous giving. In order to give radically and sacrificially—and that is the standard of giving Christ calls us to—we must have a radical confidence in the Father's provision. To downsize our house or to give away some of our retirement savings, we must truly believe that he will give us our daily bread and will reward us with eternal treasure. And "without faith it is impossible to please him" (Heb. 11:6).

The writer of Hebrews makes this connection explicit: "Keep your life free from love of money, and be content with what you have, for he has said, 'I will never leave you nor forsake you.' So we can confidently say, 'The Lord is my helper; I will not fear; what can man do to me?'" (13:5-6). Freedom from love of money starts with putting worry to death and choosing to trust in the Lord as our Helper and our Sustainer, our ever-present Provider.

Before we can ever give cheerfully, we must first receive the promise of his presence.

Ever-present Father, thank you for promising to never leave nor forsake me. I trust that you will provide for my every need. Let my trust in you overflow into a radical generosity for your kingdom. Amen.

Further reading: Hebrews 13:1-6.

Solidarity Challenge

Today I am grateful for:

1.

2.

3.

Our Father in heaven, hallowed be your name. Your kingdom come, your will be done, on earth as it is in heaven. Give us this day our daily bread, and forgive us our debts, as we also have forgiven our debtors. And lead us not into temptation, but deliver us from evil.

Trust

Little Children

"Jesus said 'Let the little children come to me and do not hinder them, for to such belongs the kingdom of heaven.'" (Matt.19:14)

Throughout Scripture, Jesus calls his disciples to be like children. In Matthew 18, Jesus says, "'Truly, I say to you, unless you turn and become like children, you will never enter the kingdom of heaven.'" What can we as disciples learn from children?

Children bring every need and want to their parents. No joy or sorrow, however trivial, is off the table. Children prattle on endlessly about their days, about everything going on in their minds and hearts.

Children practice complete dependence on their parents. When they have nightmares, they run to their parents' arms; when they're hungry, they ask their parents for food. Children don't hesitate to bring their demands to their parents. They know instinctively that they receive everything from their parents' hands.

Children take delight in the present moment. They are relentlessly concerned with the immediate and content with repetition, happy to go over the same things again and again. Often, the smallest things bring children the deepest delight.

Children are happily humble. They embody innocence and self-forgetfulness. They are unconcerned with reputation, status or power.

Children have great faith in the power of their parents. Think of the typical playground boast, "My daddy can outrun your daddy." Children trust that their parents can handle every problem and sort through every complication. When trouble comes, they turn naturally to their parents.

We who call God Father have much to imitate from children, "for to such belongs the kingdom of heaven" (Matt. 19:14).

Solidarity Challenge

Loving Father, thank you for adopting me into your family. You honor the "little children." Teach me to embody a childlike meekness, simplicity and trust, fully relying on you for every need. Amen.

Further reading: Mark 9:36-37; Matthew 18:10.

Today I am grateful for:

1.

2.

3.

Our Father in heaven, hallowed be your name. Your kingdom come, your will be done, on earth as it is in heaven. Give us this day our daily bread, and forgive us our debts, as we also have forgiven our debtors. And lead us not into temptation, but deliver us from evil.

giving

This week, give 10% of your most recent paycheck if you haven't already. You can give to your local church or to a ministry that you love.

Right now, list three things that you are anxious about and pray to God about them, out loud if you are able. Then, read Philippians 4:6–7:

Do not be anxious about anything, but in everything by prayer and supplication with thanksgiving let your requests be made known to God. And the peace of God, which surpasses all understanding, will guard your hearts and your minds in Christ Jesus.

Continue to maintain your daily practices of gratitude and prayer.

Read one daily devotional about the amazing generosity of our God.

Solidarity Challenge

The God Who Gives

"For you know the grace of our Lord Jesus Christ, that though he was rich, yet for your sake he became poor, so that you by his poverty might become rich." (2 Cor. 8:9)

The heart of the gospel is God becoming "poor" so that we might become rich—the story of God exchanging the riches of heaven for an animal feeding trough. In the Incarnation, God "emptied himself," taking the form of a servant and being born in the likeness of man (Phil. 2:7). Jesus grew up as a carpenter's son, not as the son of an esteemed rabbi or a prince in a Roman palace. "Foxes have holes, and birds of the air have nests, but the Son of Man has nowhere to lay his head," he told his followers—the God of the universe as a vagabond preacher (Luke 9:58). On earth, he continued to give: his time, his attention, his tears, his blood.

And, grace upon grace, all of it was undeserved. It's easy to give to people who love us back. But while we were still his enemies—the scorning soldiers, the unrepentant thief, the scoffing religious leaders—that's when he poured out his life for us. Grace is God gifting himself to the unworthy. "For God so loved the world, that he gave his only Son, that whoever believes in him should not perish but have eternal life" (John 3:16).

Because of this gift we're rich beyond imagination. We're seated in the heavenly places (Eph. 2:6). We're clothed with his righteousness (Isa. 61:10). We have an inheritance stored for us in heaven (1 Pet. 1:4). We are his beloved children (1 John 3:2). We have the privilege of crying out to God, "Abba! Father!" (Gal. 4:6).

Generosity begins with worship of this grace-giving, self-sacrificing, cross-bearing God. We give because he first gave to us.

Giving

Abba, Father, thank you for the precious gift of your Son Jesus Christ. Thank you for loving me in my unworthiness. Please help me to treasure your gift above all else. Amen.

Further reading: Philippians 2:1-11.

Today I am grateful for:

1.

2.

3.

Our Father in heaven, hallowed be your name. Your kingdom come, your will be done, on earth as it is in heaven. Give us this day our daily bread, and forgive us our debts, as we also have forgiven our debtors. And lead us not into temptation, but deliver us from evil.

Solidarity Challenge

Two Coins

"Jesus looked up and saw the rich putting their gifts into the offering box, and he saw a poor widow put in two small copper coins." (Luke 21:1-2)

In a world where the CEOs of Fortune 500 companies make headlines with their donations, the widow's offering presents both a comfort and a challenge. Her story reassures us because it shows that Jesus doesn't evaluate our generosity based on the quantity we've given. The rich people who donated large sums—shouldn't they have received Jesus's praise? But instead of mentioning them, Jesus directs our attention to two small copper coins.

You may think you have nothing to offer, at least by the world's standards. Maybe you're a college student struggling to pay tuition or a mother barely making ends meet. The widow's story shows that nothing is too small to be seen by God and used for his kingdom.

Still, let's not forget why Jesus commends the widow. Her offering was small but also incomparably large. A fraction of a day's labor and the entirety of her savings. Nothing and everything. For when she dropped those two coins in the temple box, she "put in all she had to live on," leaving a legacy of wholehearted surrender and sacrificial giving. Dare we follow in her footsteps?

I suspect the widow left the temple richer than anyone else, for she showed that she possessed Someone who eclipses all earthly treasure. As the biblical commentator Matthew Henry notes, the widow's generosity sprang out of a deep trust in Jehovah-Jireh, the God who provides. That same God promises us: "Do not be anxious about your life, what you will eat or what you will drink....But seek first the kingdom of God and his righteousness and all these things will be added to you" (Matt. 6:25, 33). *Offer your best, your two coins. I'll take care of the rest.*

Giving

Jehovah-Jireh, you are the God who provides. I trust that you can use my talents and treasures, no matter how insignificant they seem. Help me to trust your character and promises. And may that trust flow into sacrificial, transformational giving. Amen.

Further reading: Luke 21:1-4; Matthew 6:25-34.

Today I am grateful for:

1.

2.

3.

Our Father in heaven, hallowed be your name. Your kingdom come, your will be done, on earth as it is in heaven. Give us this day our daily bread, and forgive us our debts, as we also have forgiven our debtors. And lead us not into temptation, but deliver us from evil.

Solidarity Challenge

A Small Red Mark

"Do not lay up for yourselves treasures on earth, where moth and rust destroy and where thieves break in and steal, but lay up for yourselves treasures in heaven, where neither moth nor rust destroys and where thieves do not break in and steal." (Matt. 6:19-20)

Pastor Francis Chan wanted to show his church the weight of eternity, so he uncoiled a long rope in front of the congregation. Then, he pointed to a small red mark at the very top of the rope. That's what life on earth is like compared to eternity, he said.

Time and eternity are the backdrop for Jesus's words in this passage in Matthew 6. None of our material possessions—whether a shiny new Porsche or the latest airpods—will escape the sickle of time. Either they'll break down first or our bodies will. No consumer good will outlast the small red mark at the beginning of the rope.

But the rope continues, and so do we. We are all immortals, as C.S. Lewis explains. That's why Jesus tells us to store up treasure in heaven. It's a simple calculus, really. Trade the temporal for the eternal. Exchange the things that decay for the things that last.

How do we make this trade? By leveraging the "treasure" we've been given—the time, the talents, the money—for the kingdom of God. By spending these resources on behalf of the oppressed, the poor, the hungry and needy. By seeking God's heart as we steward our gifts.

There's no buyer's remorse in this transaction, no regrets about what we've given up. As the missionary to Ecuador Jim Elliot once said, "He is no fool who gives what he cannot keep to gain that which he cannot lose."

Everlasting God, thank you for the eternal life you've given me through your Son Jesus Christ. Help me to live every day and to weigh every purchase in light of eternity. Teach me to store up treasure in heaven instead of on earth. Amen.

Further reading: Matthew 6:19-24; John 14:1-4.

Today I am grateful for:

1.

2.

3.

Our Father in heaven, hallowed be your name. Your kingdom come, your will be done, on earth as it is in heaven. Give us this day our daily bread, and forgive us our debts, as we also have forgiven our debtors. And lead us not into temptation, but deliver us from evil.

Solidarity Challenge

Putting God to the Test

"Bring the full tithe into the storehouse, that there may be food in my house. And thereby put me to the test, says the Lord of hosts, if I will not open the windows of heaven for you and pour down for you a blessing until there is no more need." (Mal. 3:10)

Tithing is a touchy topic among Christians. We can stomach messages from our pastors on lust or pride, but we start to squirm when the sermon deals with our wallets.

But tithing matters to God. Why? Why does God care if we give 10% of our incomes? After all, he already owns the cattle on a thousand hills (Ps. 50:10).

God cares about tithing because he cares about our hearts. He knows that materialism and greed and the love of money can ravage our lives. A tithe is a regular reminder of our ultimate treasure in Christ himself—a regular injection of immunity against the plague of materialism.

But tithing also matters because generosity builds God's kingdom. When we give our money, whether to a local church or to a charity, we allow God to use our finances to advance his purposes on earth: to heal the sick, to bind up the brokenhearted and to bring good news to the poor. If God can use a widow's two coins, he can use our 10%.

Notice also God's promise. *Put me to the test,* he tells us. *I will open the windows of heaven for you.* Whether the blessing comes in the form of material resources or a closer walk with himself, God promises his favor for those who give generously.

God's promises are evergreen, as real as they were in Malachi's time. Today, will we put him to the test?

Father in heaven, you command me to put you to the test. Give me the strength and joy to bring my full tithe into the storehouse. And use that tithe for your purposes, to build your kingdom and to do your will on earth as it is in heaven. Amen.

Giving

Further reading: Malachi 3:6-12; Psalm 50:12-15.

Today I am grateful for:

1.

2.

3.

Our Father in heaven, hallowed be your name. Your kingdom come, your will be done, on earth as it is in heaven. Give us this day our daily bread, and forgive us our debts, as we also have forgiven our debtors. And lead us not into temptation, but deliver us from evil.

Solidarity Challenge

Two Masters

"You cannot serve God and money." (Matt. 6:24b)

From time to time, we all wish that Jesus was a bit more ambiguous in this passage. But he doesn't mince words. The choice is clear: God or mammon. Like Joshua speaking to the people of Israel, he tells us: "Choose this day whom you will serve" (Josh. 24:15).

Notice that he doesn't make an explicit command one way or another. Instead, he simply makes a descriptive statement about the human condition: "No one can serve two masters, for either he will hate the one and love the other, or he will be devoted to the one and despise the other" (Matt. 6:24). All humans are mastered by something or someone, Jesus seems to be saying. And to that master we devote our time, attention and affection. It could be money, fame or career. But there will be one master ruling our lives, capturing our hearts. (If you're a fan of *The Lord of the Rings*, "One ring to rule them all".)

But God is the only master truly worth serving. Saint Augustine put it this way: "You have made us for yourself, O Lord, and our heart is restless until it finds its rest in you." We are designed to run on God like a car is made to run on gasoline, said C.S. Lewis in *Mere Christianity*. To worship God is to become who we were meant to be. To serve money is to lose sight of our true selves.

And so we return to the choice: God or our pocketbooks. Let's pray that we have strength to say with Joshua, "As for me and my house, we will serve the LORD."

Lord God, you could not have made the choice clearer. Thank you for being a master who is good and gracious. Enable me to serve you and you only. Wean my heart away from money. Fasten it more tightly to yourself. Amen.

Further reading: Matthew 6:19-24; Joshua 24:14-28.

Giving

Today I am grateful for:

1.

2.

3.

Our Father in heaven, hallowed be your name. Your kingdom come, your will be done, on earth as it is in heaven. Give us this day our daily bread, and forgive us our debts, as we also have forgiven our debtors. And lead us not into temptation, but deliver us from evil.

Solidarity Challenge

Stewards

"For it will be like a man going on a journey, who called his servants and entrusted to them his property." (Matt. 25:14)

Most of us know the parable of the talents. In our reading of this parable, we tend to focus mostly on how the servants handled the talents: emulate the faithful servants, avoid the mistakes of the unfaithful one.

But, in doing so, we overlook the startling premise of this parable: the man entrusting his servants with his property. What that means, of course, is that God has entrusted us with his property. We are his stewards.

We tend to think of our money as just that—ours. Ours to save, ours to spend, ours to give. But God tells us that this money was never ours to start with. This is a hard truth to accept in our self-reliant, individualistic American culture. *Didn't I earn this money?* But Deuteronomy 8:18 has an answer: "You shall remember the LORD your God, *for it is he who gives you power to get wealth"* (italics mine).

The same can be said about our other "talents": our time and abilities, even our bodies. "You are not your own," the Apostle Paul says, for we were each bought with a price (1 Cor. 6:19). When we truly take this truth to heart—that our entire lives and selves belong to the Lord—our approach to money fundamentally changes. If our financial resources belong to God, then they must be stewarded with his purposes in mind.

We all want to be the faithful servant in this parable. But before we can be faithful, we must first recognize the true Owner of the talents.

Lord Jesus, thank you for entrusting me with talents of time, money and ability. Remind me each day that I am your steward. Teach me to be faithful with what you have entrusted to me. Amen.

Further reading: Matthew 25:14-30; Deuteronomy 8:11-20.

Giving

Today I am grateful for:

1.

2.

3.

Our Father in heaven, hallowed be your name. Your kingdom come, your will be done, on earth as it is in heaven. Give us this day our daily bread, and forgive us our debts, as we also have forgiven our debtors. And lead us not into temptation, but deliver us from evil.

Solidarity Challenge

Duty and Delight

"In all things I have shown you that by working hard in this way you must help the weak and remember the words of the Lord Jesus, how he himself said, 'It is more blessed to give than to receive.'"
(Acts 20:35)

All Christian discipleship flows from delight, and nowhere is this more evident than in the discipline of giving. It is more *blessed* to give than to receive. "God loves a *cheerful* giver," Paul says in 2 Corinthians 9:7 (italics mine). Giving should be a celebration, like dancing in the rain or waking up to the dawn of a summer holiday.

And yet, too often, we treat giving like we do turning in a school essay or paying taxes. It's not that we withhold anything from God. We pray to surrender our money. We tithe regularly. Sometimes, we even drop a little extra in the offering plate. But the crux of the matter lies at the heart level: we are merely dutiful in our obedience, when God wants us to *delight*. Too often, we are more like Ebenezer Scrooge than like Zacchaeus joyfully offering half of his possessions to the poor. But we deprive ourselves when we give grudgingly instead of with a smile and a skip in our step.

How do we find such joy in generosity? Only by embracing the preciousness of Jesus. The same Paul who shared these words in Acts also wrote this to the Philippian church: "I count everything as loss because of the surpassing worth of knowing Christ Jesus my Lord" (Phil. 3:8).

We can give freely and happily because we know that all we ever need, now or in the future, has been bought for us on the Cross of Calvary. Delight in Christ is the fountainhead of joyful giving. "Thanks be to God for his inexpressible gift!" (2 Cor. 9:15).

Father, thank you for the most amazing gift, your Son Jesus Christ. Thank you that we can know him and the power of his resurrection.

Giving

Lord, fill my heart with a holy joy so that I would know the truth of your words, "It is more blessed to give than to receive." Amen.

Further reading: Acts 20:17-35; 2 Corinthians 9:6-15.

Today I am grateful for:

1.

2.

3.

Our Father in heaven, hallowed be your name. Your kingdom come, your will be done, on earth as it is in heaven. Give us this day our daily bread, and forgive us our debts, as we also have forgiven our debtors. And lead us not into temptation, but deliver us from evil.

fasting

This week, pick one day to fast for a twenty-four-hour period and commit to it.* This is the only day of fasting in the Solidarity Challenge.

Right now, list three things that you are anxious about and pray to God about them, out loud if you are able. Then, read Philippians 4:6–7:

Do not be anxious about anything, but in everything by prayer and supplication with thanksgiving let your requests be made known to God. And the peace of God, which surpasses all understanding, will guard your hearts and your minds in Christ Jesus.

In addition to your day-long fast, continue to give 10% of your income and maintain your daily practices of gratitude and prayer.

Read one daily devotional about fasting.

*A note on fasting: If you have never fasted before, don't be intimidated by the practice. One good way to fast is from lunch to lunch so that you only have to miss two meals (dinner and breakfast). Make sure to drink lots of water, and you may want to also drink fruit juice. If you are unable to fast from food for medical reasons, consider giving up another daily habit like coffee-drinking or sweets.

Fasting

Fasting in the Wilderness: Part I

"O God, you are my God; earnestly I seek you" (Ps. 63:1)

Desire for God is the mother of fasting.

Like David, we often find ourselves in the wilderness—surrounded by a wasteland of hurried habits, endless meetings and pinging iPhone notifications that leave our souls hungry and parched. "My soul thirsts for you," David prays. "My flesh faints for you, as in a dry and weary land where there is no water." And so, we fast, inviting God to replenish us with himself. "Christian fasting," according to John Piper, "is the hunger of a homesickness for God."

But there are also times where we don't desire God. Times where we desire a myriad of other things instead: food, friends, work or play. Even the best gifts in life—especially the best ones—can distract us from the Giver. As our desire for God becomes crowded out by a cacophony of other desires, we begin worshipping created things instead of the Creator. To borrow C. S. Lewis's analogy, we start playing with mud pies when we're offered a holiday at the sea.

Fasting reorients our desires towards God. As we fast, we invite the Lord to sharpen our appetite for himself. We feel the pangs of physical hunger and the tremors of a holy longing. We return to worshipping the living God. As Piper puts it, "When God is the supreme hunger of our hearts, he will be supreme in everything."

To fast is to be awakened to the One who calls himself the Living Water and the Bread of Life. Oh, that we might hunger and thirst for him!

Oh God, you are my God. My soul longs for you. Teach me to fast. Awaken in me a deeper longing for yourself. You are my deepest joy. Amen.

Further reading: Psalm 63:1-11; Psalm 42:1-11.

Solidarity Challenge

Today I am grateful for:

1.

2.

3.

Our Father in heaven, hallowed be your name. Your kingdom come, your will be done, on earth as it is in heaven. Give us this day our daily bread, and forgive us our debts, as we also have forgiven our debtors. And lead us not into temptation, but deliver us from evil.

Fasting

Fasting in the Wilderness: Part II

"Your steadfast love is better than life" (Ps. 63:3)

If desire is the root of fasting, delight is its fruit. We fast knowing that God himself brings ultimate joy. "My soul will be satisfied as with fat and rich food," David prays. Think about eating and relishing your favorite meal—that's what it feels like to have our souls feast on God.

Fasting, like every other spiritual discipline, is simply a pathway, a means to an ultimate end. C. S. Lewis made this point in "The Weight of Glory": "The New Testament has lots to say about self-denial, but not about self-denial as an end in itself." We fast in order to know and enjoy God more fully—a God who is infinitely valuable and supremely satisfying.

Like the Apostle Paul, we must become entranced with our Lord: "I count everything as loss because of the surpassing worth of knowing Christ Jesus my Lord. For his sake I have suffered the loss of all things and count them as rubbish, in order that I may gain Christ" (Phil. 3:8). We are made for God, and only he can truly satisfy our souls.

When we see fasting as a discipline to know God more deeply, we lose the cloud of gloomy asceticism and sanctimonious self-pity that so often broods over those who fast. We're not really renouncing anything, after all; we're simply baring our souls for a closer encounter with God. And that encounter causes our souls to sing, "For you have been my help, and in the shadow of your wings I will sing for joy" (Ps. 63:7).

Sustaining God, satisfy me in the morning with your steadfast love. As I fast, help me to delight more deeply in you, for only you can truly satisfy. Amen.

Further reading: Philippians 3:7-11.

Solidarity Challenge

Today I am grateful for:

1.

2.

3.

Our Father in heaven, hallowed be your name. Your kingdom come, your will be done, on earth as it is in heaven. Give us this day our daily bread, and forgive us our debts, as we also have forgiven our debtors. And lead us not into temptation, but deliver us from evil.

Fasting

When You Fast

*"And when you fast, do not look gloomy like the hypocrites, for they
disfigure their faces that their fasting may be seen by others."*
(Matt. 6:16)

Fasting sometimes seems like a discipline reserved for the spiritual elite. Sure, fasting is great for a Benedictine monk cloistered from the world. But to fast in our modern, busy lives—with meetings to attend, children to care for, fitness routines to fulfill—is that possible?

Like every discipline Jesus practiced, fasting isn't meant for the spiritual aristocracy. In this passage from the Sermon on the Mount, Jesus shows that he expects his followers to fast: not "if" you fast, but "when."

True, fasting is difficult. It grates against our natural appetites and daily rhythms. But, as disciples of Christ, we can't pick and choose from Jesus's teachings. Discipleship, after all, means taking up our cross and following the crucified Christ. As Richard Foster puts it in a chapter on fasting from *The Celebration of Discipline*, "Have we become so accustomed to 'cheap grace' that we instinctively shy away from more demanding calls to obedience?"

As we fast, we should always be on guard against that most dangerous of vices: spiritual pride. Jesus condemns the "hypocrites" for fasting in order to appear more religious to others. Fasting is a bridge between our hearts and God's. Such things are best done in secret (Matt. 6:18). God sees and rewards, and that is enough.

*Father, thank you for the gift of fasting. Help me to carve out times
to fast even on busy days with hectic schedules. Teach me to fast with
a heart of humility. Amen.*

Further reading: Matthew 6:16-18; Mark 2:18-20.

Solidarity Challenge

Today I am grateful for:

1.

2.

3.

Our Father in heaven, hallowed be your name. Your kingdom come, your will be done, on earth as it is in heaven. Give us this day our daily bread, and forgive us our debts, as we also have forgiven our debtors. And lead us not into temptation, but deliver us from evil.

Fasting

Bread

"Man shall not live by bread alone, but by every word that comes from the mouth of God." (Matt. 4:4)

Just as bread feeds our bodies, God's Word nourishes our souls. In Scripture we find a trove of riches: commands to guide our lives, promises to comfort our hearts, truths to remind us of who we are and why we are here.

In Psalm 119, the psalmist says, "How sweet are your words to my taste, sweeter than honey to my mouth!" Jeremiah the prophet says something similar: "Your words were found, and I ate them, and your words became to me a joy and the delight of my heart" (Jer. 15:16).

And yet, instead of feasting on God's Word, we so often snack casually on it. I love food (especially bread!), and so I never skip meals, even when I'm tired or feeling lazy. In contrast, when my life gets hectic, my time in Scripture is often the first thing to get cut from my schedule—to the detriment of my entire being. Just as our bodies decline without food, our souls decay without spiritual nourishment.

Fasting reminds us of the source of true sustenance: we live on every word that comes from the mouth of God. It's no coincidence that Jesus said these words to the tempter after fasting for forty days. Fasting molds our hearts and shapes our appetites so that we find our deepest delight in God and in his Word. Jesus made this point to his disciples in John 4, when his disciples were urging him to eat: "Jesus said to them, 'My food is to do the will of Him who sent me and to accomplish His work.'"

Father, thank you for your word in Scripture and for the Word, Jesus Christ. Shape my heart to hunger for your word and to feed on your promises, for you are the sustenance of my soul. Amen.

Further reading: John 4:31-45; Psalm 119:97-104.

Solidarity Challenge

Today I am grateful for:

1.

2.

3.

Our Father in heaven, hallowed be your name. Your kingdom come, your will be done, on earth as it is in heaven. Give us this day our daily bread, and forgive us our debts, as we also have forgiven our debtors. And lead us not into temptation, but deliver us from evil.

Fasting

True Fasting

"Is not this the fast that I choose: to loose the bonds of wickedness, to undo the straps of the yoke, to let the oppressed go free, and to break every yoke?" (Isa. 58:6)

Most of us fast expecting to return to stocked pantries and full refrigerators. But millions around the world don't have this luxury. According to the United Nations, over 800 million people go about daily life without enough to eat. Our hunger is a choice; for countless others, it's a harsh reality.

By fasting, we practice solidarity with those who suffer from hunger and malnutrition. Pastor Darren Rouanzoin puts it this way: "When we choose this fast, we choose to allow our bodies to feel hunger, and this hunger becomes an act of solidarity with those who are hungry by no choice of their own. We align our bodies to connect with those suffering."

In this sense, fasting embodies a fundamental biblical truth: walking humbly with God is always accompanied by seeking justice and loving mercy. Our vertical relationship with God transforms our horizontal relationships with others. We fast for a closer communion with God, but we also fast to cultivate a heart of solidarity with the poor, broken and hurting around the world.

False fasting divorces the horizontal from the vertical—preserving an aura of religiosity while neglecting God's heart for the oppressed. God condemns this kind of fasting in Isaiah 58: "Fasting like yours this day will not make your voice to be heard on high" (Isa. 58:4). In contrast, true fasting both draws us to the divine and propels us outward: "Is it not to share your bread with the hungry and bring the homeless poor into your house; when you see the naked, to cover him, and not to hide yourself from your own flesh?" (Isa. 58:7).

Biblical fasting is both a spiritual discipline and a source of social transformation.

Solidarity Challenge

Father, you are a God who is high and lifted up, but you also dwell with the poor and the broken. As I fast, mold my heart and break it for what breaks yours. Help me to practice true fasting. Amen.

Further reading: Isaiah 58:1-14; Micah 6:1-8.

Today I am grateful for:

1.

2.

3.

Our Father in heaven, hallowed be your name. Your kingdom come, your will be done, on earth as it is in heaven. Give us this day our daily bread, and forgive us our debts, as we also have forgiven our debtors. And lead us not into temptation, but deliver us from evil.

DAY THIRTY-FOUR

Rend Your Hearts

"'Yet even now,' declares the Lord, 'return to me with all your heart, with fasting, with weeping, and with mourning; and rend your hearts and not your garments.'" (Joel 2:12-14)

As Christians, we're forgiven by God because of the death and resurrection of Jesus Christ. But even as we grow in righteousness, we still grapple with sin in our daily lives. We forget or ignore the promises and commands of God; we fall into old habits of lust, greed and pride. As a result, repentance should be a daily practice for followers of Jesus.

Fasting is one way to practice repentance. As we fast, we confess our sins to God and invite him to expose and convict us of the rebellious habits in our lives. Fasting doesn't earn God's forgiveness or make us any more justified in his sight. But, by the Spirit's power, fasting can help us break patterns of sin and enter more fully into the abundant life Jesus has prepared for us.

Fasting can also be a powerful way to express repentance at the communal and national levels. We know that God cares about kingdoms, rulers and politics. He's involved in history and directs the fate of nations, and so we fast to seek God's favor and mercy for our country. Indeed, we have much to repent of: racial injustice, greed, a culture of lust and idolatry, among many other things.

As we fast, both individually and communally, we must remember God's call to rend our hearts and not our garments. Outward signs of repentance must always reflect an inward change. Repentance begins in the heart.

Father in heaven, thank you for your promise that if I confess my sins, you are faithful and just to forgive. Lord, I repent of all the ways I have strayed from you. Lead me back to yourself. Rend my heart, and then bind it more closely to you. Amen.

Solidarity Challenge

Further reading: Jonah 3:1-10; Joel 2:12-17.

Today I am grateful for:

1.

2.

3.

Our Father in heaven, hallowed be your name. Your kingdom come, your will be done, on earth as it is in heaven. Give us this day our daily bread, and forgive us our debts, as we also have forgiven our debtors. And lead us not into temptation, but deliver us from evil.

Friends of the Bridegroom

"When the bridegroom is taken… then they will fast." (Matt. 9:15)

John's disciples were confused. Why were they fasting while Jesus's disciples were freely eating and drinking?

I love Jesus's answer: "Can the wedding guests mourn as long as the bridegroom is with them?" Being in the presence of Jesus is like being at a wedding—a time for joy and celebration. John the Baptist recognized this: "The friend of the bridegroom, who stands and hears him, rejoices greatly at the bridegroom's voice. Therefore, this joy of mine is now complete" (John 3:29). As Christians, we are all friends of the bridegroom, and we rejoice in knowing him.

But Jesus also told of a time when the bridegroom would be "taken away." Those days are upon us. Though we share in the Spirit of Christ, Jesus has ascended to heaven and is no longer physically with us. We can't cling to him like Mary or laugh with him over a meal of broiled fish. We live in the "already" but "not yet," between the Resurrection and the renewal of all things, between the inauguration of Christ's kingdom and his final coronation. "And then they will fast": waiting and fasting are inseparable.

Fasting is born out of a longing for the bridegroom—that "homesickness for God" pastor John Piper talks about. We fast knowing that we live in a broken and hungry world, a world where image-bearers of God are trafficked and nations go to war, a world that is "groaning together in the pains of childbirth" (Rom. 8:22).

But we also fast with hope. One day, God will birth a new heaven and a new earth. He promises to eradicate all evil, wipe away every tear and make his dwelling among us. "Weeping may tarry for the night, but joy comes with the morning" (Ps. 30:5).

The bridegroom will return.

Solidarity Challenge

Until that day, we wait, we love, we serve, we cry and we fast, our hearts full of a hope that does not disappoint. "Surely, I am coming soon," he says (Rev. 22:20). And so, we pray:

Amen. Come, Lord Jesus.

Further reading: John 3:22-36; Revelation 22:1-21.

Today I am grateful for:

1.

2.

3.

Our Father in heaven, hallowed be your name. Your kingdom come, your will be done, on earth as it is in heaven. Give us this day our daily bread, and forgive us our debts, as we also have forgiven our debtors. And lead us not into temptation, but deliver us from evil.

abundance

Right now, list three things that you are anxious about and pray to God about them, out loud if you are able. Then, read Philippians 4:6–7:

Do not be anxious about anything, but in everything by prayer and supplication with thanksgiving let your requests be made known to God. And the peace of God, which surpasses all understanding, will guard your hearts and your minds in Christ Jesus.

Continue to give 10% of your income and maintain your daily practices of gratitude and prayer.

Read one daily devotional to reflect on how these practices produce abundance.

Solidarity Challenge

Abundant Giving

"From his abundance we have all received one gracious blessing after another." (John 1:16) (NLT)

Generosity is both the fruit and the root of abundant life.

Generosity leads to abundance. Left unchecked, wealth and material goods will squelch our joy and our peace. But generosity helps us experience that elusive thing called contentment. Find a person who is radically generous—I guarantee you they will be one of the most joyful people you have ever met. They will have taken to heart Jesus's words: "It is more blessed to give than to receive" (Acts 20:35).

But Jesus's commands are never meant to be merely about ourselves. We are a family of God, the Body of Christ. Abundance should always be outward-focused. When we give generously of our time, energy and resources, we help others experience physical, spiritual and emotional flourishing.

Just as abundant life is a holistic thing, generosity is more than just 10% of our paychecks. Generosity is about how we structure our schedules: how we organize our moments and our days (after all, as Annie Dillard put it, "How we spend our days is...how we spend our lives"). Generosity is about how we view other people: as tools for our advancement or as precious image-bearers of God. And, ultimately, generosity is about our hearts: who or what do we most cherish and love?

Generosity also flows from abundance: grace begets grace. People who recognize how much they have received from God, and how much they possess *in* God, will give freely and joyfully. Those who know the abundance of God—the "breadth and length and height and depth" of the love of Christ—will show tangible love to others (Eph. 3:18). We've all received "grace upon grace" (John 1:16). How can we be miserly when we've been given the greatest gift?

Abundance

Generous God, thank you for your grace in my life. You don't treat me as my sins deserve, but as far as the east is from the west, so far have you removed my transgressions from me. You are so, so good. Help me to overflow in grace and abundance toward others. Amen.

Further reading: John 1.

Today I am grateful for:

1.

2.

3.

Our Father in heaven, hallowed be your name. Your kingdom come, your will be done, on earth as it is in heaven. Give us this day our daily bread, and forgive us our debts, as we also have forgiven our debtors. And lead us not into temptation, but deliver us from evil.

Solidarity Challenge

Abundant Prayer

"I am the vine; you are the branches. Whoever abides in me and I in him, he it is that bears much fruit, for apart from me you can do nothing." (John 15:5)

A life of abundance comes from abiding deeply in Jesus. In the hours before he was about to be crucified, Jesus shared a meal with his disciples and gave them his final teachings. "Abide in me, and I in you," he told them, and he tells us the same today. Apart from abiding in Christ, we are severed branches—dry, brittle and barren. But when we abide in Christ, he works in us to bear his fruit.

To abide is an act of revolution in today's restless, hurried world. We neglect silence, solitude and stillness—the very things that make abiding possible. But, for the Christian, abiding is not optional; it's our lifeblood.

What does it mean to abide? To abide is to commune with the Lord, to fellowship with him, to heed his voice to "Come away by yourselves to a desolate place and rest a while" (Mark 6:31). Abiding requires prayer, both pouring out our hearts before the Lord and—perhaps more important in today's world—dwelling in stillness before him, listening for his "gentle whisper" (1 Kgs. 19:12).

When we abide in Christ, as a branch growing out of the vine, our desires become identified with his. We begin to pray for the same things that Jesus prays for, and the Father delights to answer those requests. "If you abide in me, and my words abide in you, ask whatever you wish, and it will be done for you" (John 15:7). Prayer that is born out of abiding leads to true abundance: "Ask and you will receive, that your joy may be full" (John 16:24).

Christ is the Vine. But, as Hudson Taylor, the missionary to China, once wrote, "Jesus is not that alone—he is soil and sunshine, air and showers, and ten thousand times more than we have ever dreamed, wished for or needed."

Abundance

He is the source of our abundance.

Jesus, True Vine, I can do nothing apart from you. You are my strength, my song and my salvation. Teach me to abide, Lord. Draw me deeper into yourself. Amen.

Further reading: John 15.

Today I am grateful for:

1.

2.

3.

Our Father in heaven, hallowed be your name. Your kingdom come, your will be done, on earth as it is in heaven. Give us this day our daily bread, and forgive us our debts, as we also have forgiven our debtors. And lead us not into temptation, but deliver us from evil.

Abundant Fasting

"I'll provide abundance for those who are weary, and fill all who are faint." (Jer. 31:25) (ISV)

Fasting can feel like the antithesis of abundance. Intentionally setting aside food or other good things in life seems, at first glance, to be ascetic rather than abundant. How do we experience fullness while feeling the growls of an empty stomach?

But, as Saint Augustine explained, true abundance comes when our loves are rightly ordered. When we allow the counterfeit gods of money or power or success to take the place of God in our hearts, we miss out on a life infused with freedom, joy and the presence of the Lord. That's why Jesus told the crowds that he was the Bread of Life, the manna sent from heaven. That's why he cried out, "If anyone thirsts, let him come to me and drink" (John 7:37). Unless we eat of this Bread and drink of this Water, we will never know abundant life.

Fasting reorders our affections. As we fast, the Spirit of Christ works in us to expose the idols of our hearts and to direct our desires to himself. Fasting is a God-ordained pruning of the heart.

Is it really surprising that God would work through fasting to produce abundance? After all, when Jesus announced the kingdom of heaven, he heralded the entrance of the Great Reversal. Greatness now comes through servanthood. Finding treasure requires letting go. Life requires death, and baptism starts with burial. Glory is a bleeding man on a cross.

Like all good things in life, abundance is costly. But even as we fast, as we hunger and thirst and surrender our longings to the Lord, we do so with fullness. We remember that the ultimate sacrifice has already been made.

Abundance

Father, thank you for the gift of your Son—the Bread of Life and the Living Water. I hunger and thirst for more of you, O God. Let me drink deeply of you today. Amen.

Further reading: Psalm 63.

Today I am grateful for:

1.

2.

3.

Our Father in heaven, hallowed be your name. Your kingdom come, your will be done, on earth as it is in heaven. Give us this day our daily bread, and forgive us our debts, as we also have forgiven our debtors. And lead us not into temptation, but deliver us from evil.

Solidarity Challenge

Abundant Gratitude

"Blessed are the poor in spirit, for theirs is the kingdom of heaven."
(Matt. 5:3)

In a chapter of *Pilgrim at Tinker Creek* called "Seeing," Annie Dillard tells the story of how as a child she would take a penny from her collection and hide it near a tree or in a crevice in the sidewalk. Then, she would draw arrows pointing to the coin: "SURPRISE AHEAD or MONEY THIS WAY."

"The world is fairly studded and strewn with pennies cast broadside from a generous hand," Dillard writes. "But—and this is the point—who gets excited by a mere penny? ... It is dire poverty indeed when a man is so malnourished and fatigued that he won't stoop to pick up a penny. But if you cultivate a healthy poverty and simplicity, so that finding a penny will literally make your day, then, since the world is in fact planted in pennies, you have with your poverty bought a lifetime of days. It is that simple. What you see is what you get."

God has indeed strewn the world with "pennies"—everyday, pedestrian gifts that we so easily overlook or take for granted—like the patter of the rain, the warmth of a smile or the brilliant hues of a sunset. So often, we are too spiritually or physically fatigued to appreciate these blessings. We've given up on abundance. We've lost the ability to see.

Christ-infused, Spirit-driven gratitude helps us recover our sight. How are we to "give thanks," as God commands in Scripture, unless we are on the lookout for things to be thankful for? Gratitude helps us see the abundance hidden in plain sight.

Gratitude brings abundance by helping us cultivate a poverty of spirit. To be poor in spirit is to embrace total dependence—to be perpetually in wonder at the riches of God's grace. Such people see the world as bursting with pennies, strewn by a holy and forgiving God. It is to the penny collectors that Jesus gives the kingdom of heaven.

Abundance

Lavish God, you are so good. Thank you for the everyday gifts that I so often take for granted. Thank you for the pennies. Lord, open my eyes each day so that I don't miss them. Amen.

Further reading: Matthew 5.

Today I am grateful for:

1.

2.

3.

Our Father in heaven, hallowed be your name. Your kingdom come, your will be done, on earth as it is in heaven. Give us this day our daily bread, and forgive us our debts, as we also have forgiven our debtors. And lead us not into temptation, but deliver us from evil.

Solidarity Challenge

Abundant Trust

"I have said these things to you, that in me you may have peace."
(John 16:33)

Abundant life is easy on paper. It becomes a lot trickier when we're dealing with a hectic work schedule, a sickly body or an unfaithful spouse. Is abundant life really possible in the nitty gritty of everyday life?

It must be possible—otherwise, we're without hope. These are the lives we live: not some carefree existence, but stories full of ruptured promises, spiraling anxieties and unfulfilled longings. Again and again, the brokenness of the world intrudes.

But so does Jesus.

He intruded into our world 2,000 years ago as a Jewish baby born in a manger. This Jesus, the Son of God and Son of Man, walked among us. He toiled for thirty years in the mundane. He got hungry and thirsty and tired. He wept over lost loved ones. He knew intimate friendship and tasted bitter betrayal. He went through that most human of experiences—death. And, in his dying, he redeemed for us *this* day—this routine, unextraordinary day with its worries and doubts and gifts. As Tish Harrison Warren explains, "Today is the proving ground of what I believe and of whom I worship."

And so, the abundant life begins with this abundant day, this abundant hour, this abundant moment. It starts with trusting Jesus's promise that he is "with us always" (Matt. 28:20), that he is walking with us in the grainy details of our lives, that in this very moment he is shouldering our burdens, listening to our cries and tending to our harried hearts.

The life Jesus invites us into isn't an easy one. He doesn't promise prosperity, health or a comfortable retirement. "In the world, you will have tribulation," Jesus told his disciples (John 16:33).

Abundance

But with the same breath he also said this: "Take heart! I have overcome the world."

Today, Jesus offers us abundant life. A life of joyful giving and sacrificial service, of radical love and of prayerful dependence. A life overflowing with himself.

Lord God, I rejoice in your promise of abundant life. You are the strength of my heart and my portion forever. I love you. Today, in this mundane moment, I come before you once again, hungry and broken. I choose your yoke and your way. I choose your kingdom and your will. I choose you. Amen.

Further reading: John 16.

Today I am grateful for:

1.

2.

3.

Our Father in heaven, hallowed be your name. Your kingdom come, your will be done, on earth as it is in heaven. Give us this day our daily bread, and forgive us our debts, as we also have forgiven our debtors. And lead us not into temptation, but deliver us from evil.

How have you experienced abundant life during the Solidarity Challenge? What new things did God teach you? Journal your thoughts below.

_____

_____

_____

_____

_____

_____

_____

_____

_____

_____

_____

_____

_____

_____

_____

_____

what's next?

Consider committing to these life-giving practices for an additional year. Order your copy of the Solidarity Resolution today.

This new resource from Simple Charity will be made available in 2021 on our online store. Check out simplecharity.org for more information.